A book
*is a present you can open
again and again*.

THIS BOOK BELONGS TO

FROM

# When Dinosaurs Walked

Written by Andrew Chaikin

Illustrated by Patricia Wynne

**World Book, Inc.**
a Scott Fetzer company
Chicago   London   Sydney   Toronto

Printed in the United States of America
ISBN 0-7166-1620-3
Library of Congress Catalog Card No. 91-65749

8  9  10  11  12  13  14  15  99  98  97  96

Cover design by Rosa Cabrera
Book design by Mary-Ann Lupa

*When Dinosaurs Walked* has been recommended
as scientifically and artistically accurate by The
Dinosaur Society's Book Review Committee. The
Dinosaur Society is a nonprofit corporation for the
advancement of dinosaur research, education, and art.

Once, long ago, giant animals could
make the ground shake when they walked.
Flying reptiles soared through the air. Some
great beasts had teeth longer than your
hand. Who were these creatures? Dinosaurs,
of course—and other reptiles! Millions of
years ago, they ruled the earth.

When reptiles ruled, the earth was different. It may have been warmer and wetter than it is today. There were no people back then, but dinosaurs were all around. What were the dinosaurs like? How do we know about them?

Some of their teeth, bones, and eggs have been found inside layers of rock. These parts are called fossils. Scientists use fossils as clues to figure out what the dinosaurs were like. Let's step back into the days of the dinosaurs.

Here is a herd of Apatosauruses. They were giant plant-eating dinosaurs. The sound of their footsteps probably echoed like thunder. One fully grown Apatosaurus

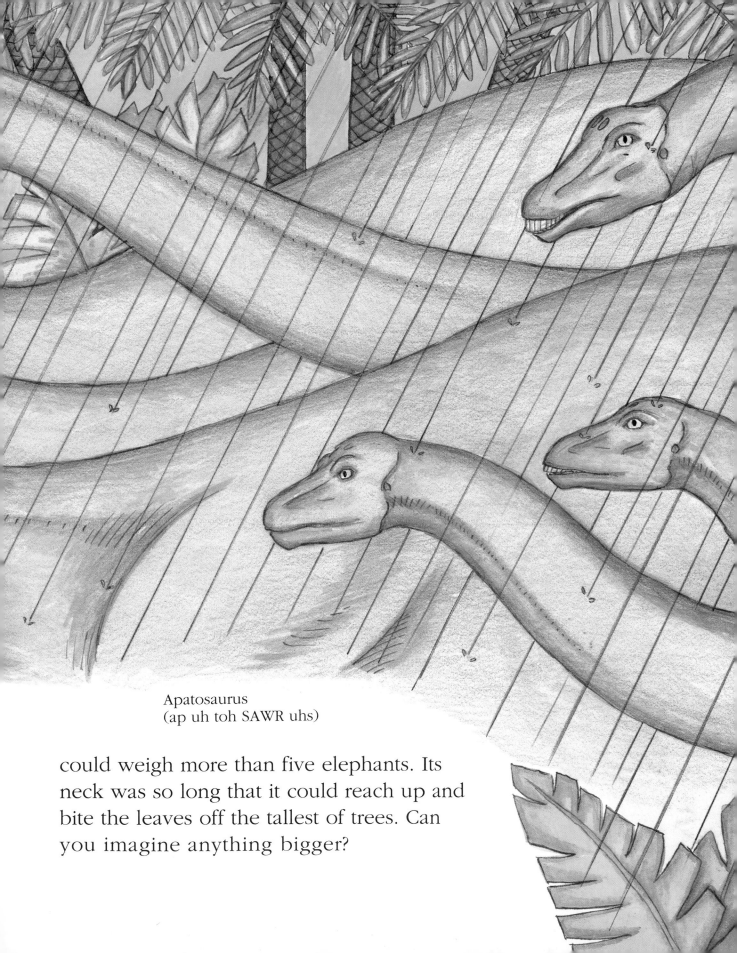

Apatosaurus
(ap uh toh SAWR uhs)

could weigh more than five elephants. Its
neck was so long that it could reach up and
bite the leaves off the tallest of trees. Can
you imagine anything bigger?

A few years ago, a scientist discovered some bones from one of the biggest dinosaurs ever found. This dinosaur was named Ultrasaurus. "Ultra" means "greatest possible." This enormous beast may have been five times larger than Apatosaurus.

Scientists think that Ultrasaurus was a gentle animal. Probably, it traveled in herds roaming the plains looking for leaves and fruits to eat from the tallest trees.

Ultrasaurus
(uhl truh SAWR uhs)

Not all dinosaurs were huge like Apatosaurus and Ultrasaurus. Compsognathus, one of the smallest dinosaurs, was no bigger than a chicken. Could such a small dinosaur have made a good pet? Probably not! Compsognathus had a mouth full of sharp teeth. It would dart around swiftly, looking for its next meal, probably a small lizard.

Compsognathus
(kahmp suh NAY thus)

How do we know which dinosaurs ate plants and which ate other animals? Their teeth give a clue. Scientists have been able to tell what different dinosaurs ate by studying fossils of their teeth.

Look at the teeth of Apatosaurus. They are flat on the ends and shaped like pegs, like the teeth of a cow. Since we know that cows eat plants, Apatosaurus probably did, also.

The teeth of Allosaurus are sharp, like a lion's. Lions are meat-eaters. What do you think Allosaurus ate?

Today, on the plains of Africa, an unlucky giraffe may end up as dinner for a hungry lion. In the time of the dinosaurs, hungry meat-eaters like Allosaurus may have hunted plant-caters like Apatosaurus. The big plant-eater was probably too slow to run away.

How do we know this? Scientists found the bones of an Apatosaurus next to the bones of an Allosaurus. The Allosaurus' teeth marks could still be seen in the Apatosaurus' tail. That Apatosaurus became dinner for Allosaurus.

Allosaurus
(al uh SAWR uhs)

Tyrannosaurus
(tih RAN uh sawr uhs)

One dinosaur was perhaps the fiercest beast of all time. Do you know which dinosaur it was? Tyrannosaurus Rex, of course. Imagine three tall people today standing on top of one another. That's about as tall as Tyrannosaurus, who also had a mouth full of sharp, jagged teeth and hooklike claws.

How could the plant-eaters protect themselves from Tyrannosaurus? Some couldn't. But the small, fast ones could run away. And other dinosaurs had protection. Look at Triceratops' three horns and that bony shield around its neck. How do you think Triceratops protected itself?

Triceratops
(try SEHR uh tahps)

Ankylosaurus was a dinosaur with a different kind of protection. Its body was covered with hard, bony knobs and spikes. Ankylosaurus' tail ended in a bony club that it could use like a weapon. One swing of that clubbed tail could have been enough to scare most enemies off.

Ankylosaurus
(an KY luh sawr uhs)

Elasmosaurus
(ih laz muh SAWR uhs)

While dinosaurs walked the land, other reptiles lived in the seas of long ago.

Look at Elasmosaurus. This creature used its long neck to lunge at fast-moving fish. Its mouth was full of sharp teeth.

Mosasaurus looked a little like a crocodile, but instead of feet, it had flippers for swimming. Its long, powerful tail helped guide it through the water.

Mosasaurus
(MOH suh sawr uhs)

Back when the dinosaurs walked the land, there were different kinds of flying reptiles, too. Pteranodon had a body about the size of a turkey, but its wings spread hugely apart—about 26 feet. That's about as much distance as four tall people lying head to foot! Can you imagine such a creature, swooping down to the water to catch fish?

And then there was the smaller Pterodactylus, no bigger than a robin. With its leathery wings, do you think Pterodactylus looks something like a bat? This reptile probably snapped up insects with its long jaws.

Pteranodon
(tehr AN uh dahn)

Pterodactylus
(tehr uh DAK
tuh luhs)

For a time, another creature shared the skies with the flying reptiles. Here is Archaeopteryx. In some ways it was like the reptiles, because it had teeth. But Archaeopteryx was covered with feathers—unlike any dinosaur or other reptile. Doesn't Archaeopteryx look like a bird? Scientists call it the first known bird.

Archaeopteryx
(ahr kee AHP tuhr ihks)

Today, no dinosaurs shake the ground as they walk. No flying reptiles soar. These creatures, and others, are gone. What happened to them? Some scientists think that a meteorite—a huge chunk of rock from space—crashed into the earth. The crash might have kicked up a thick cloud of dust. The dust might have blocked the sun's light and heat.

Other scientists think that dinosaurs died off slowly, over a long period of time. They think that the earth was growing colder and the dinosaurs could not live in the new climate.

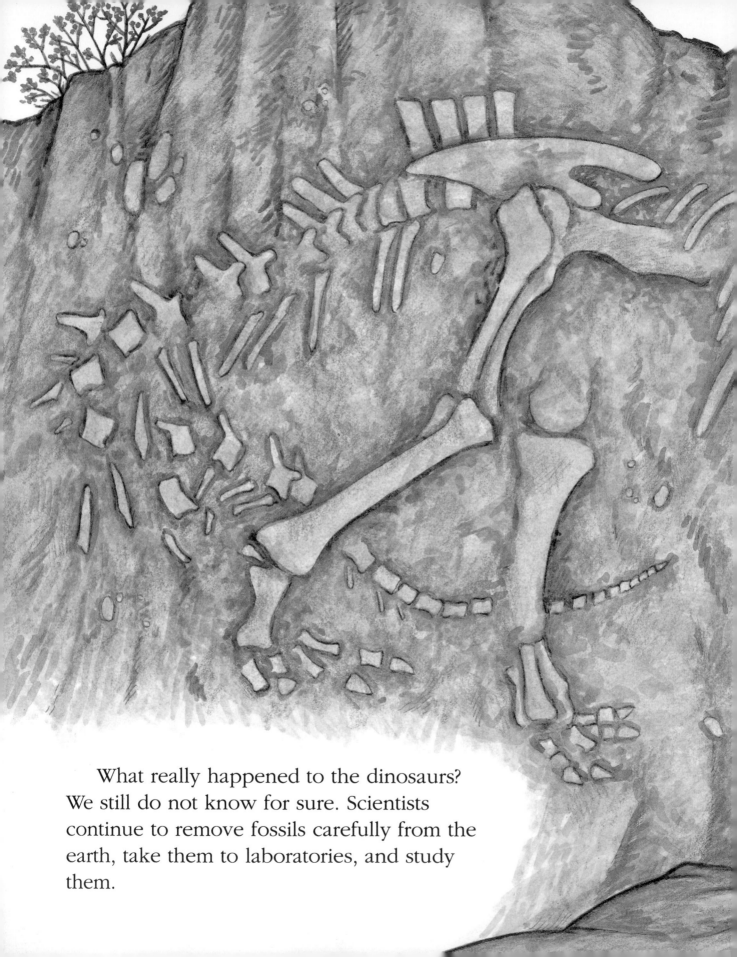

What really happened to the dinosaurs?
We still do not know for sure. Scientists
continue to remove fossils carefully from the
earth, take them to laboratories, and study
them.

What will they find out? Every discovery tells us something. Maybe the bones tell of a new kind of early reptile. Maybe they tell us more about how the dinosaurs lived and what happened to them. There is still so much to learn about those long-ago days when dinosaurs walked the earth.

Is it a dinosaur, a flying reptile, or a swimming reptile?

Is it a meat-eating dinosaur or a plant-eating dinosaur?

## More About Dinosaurs

When the dinosaurs lived, the continents were not separate as they are today. They were joined together in one huge "super continent." Later, the continents broke apart, and today we find dinosaur fossils on every continent.

For many years, scientists assumed dinosaurs, like modern reptiles, were cold-blooded. That would have meant they were slow-moving beasts. Today, scientists believe some dinosaurs were warm-blooded like mammals and were capable of running and moving vigorously.

Most dinosaurs probably laid eggs like modern reptiles. But unlike reptiles, at least some dinosaurs cared for their young the way birds do. They kept nests and brought back food for the babies to eat. Fossil nests with eggs and baby dinosaurs have been found in the Western United States.

Apatosaurus may have eaten between 500 and 2,000 pounds of plants every day! Huge Ultrasaurus was so big that scientists wonder if it had to eat all the time just to stay alive.

Tyrannosaurus' arms were so short that they could not reach its mouth. Scientists wonder what they were used for. Some believe they may have helped Tyrannosaurus push itself to a standing position after lying down or sleeping.

## To Parents

Children delight in hearing and reading about dinosaurs. *When Dinosaurs Walked* will provide your child with interesting information about a number of dinosaurs and other prehistoric animals, as well as a bridge into learning some important concepts. Here are a few easy and natural ways your child can express feelings and understandings about the animals in the book. You know your child and can best judge which ideas he or she will enjoy most.

Cereal dinosaurs are fun to make (but they can't be eaten)! Help your child make an outline of one of the dinosaurs. Have your child cover the shape with glue and then pat the cereal into place. Glue on colored paper pieces to add eyes, ears, or other details.

Did your child have a favorite prehistoric animal? Look through the book together to find a picture of it. After reading the description, have your child use clay or play dough to make a model.

Your child will enjoy making a dinosaur book to show to other family members. Print the name of a dinosaur or other prehistoric animal on each page. Your child may then draw pictures of the animals on the pages. Older children may write short descriptions of the animals on the backs of the pages.

Children enjoy saying the names of dinosaurs and other creatures, and will have a good time playing a name-chain game.

Begin by saying the name of a dinosaur or other animal in the book. Have your child repeat that name and say the name of another creature. The next player says the name of the first two animals and gives a third name. The play continues until a player can no longer remember the names given. Start again with a new name. Each time, try to build a longer list.

Make a "fossil" print. Scientists discover objects from the past by finding fossils. Leaves and shells make good prints. Press a 1-inch layer of play dough into a small pie plate. Press the leaf or shell down on the dough to leave a print. Remove the leaf or shell. Mix equal parts of plaster of Paris and water, and pour the mixture over the play dough. Let the plaster set for 4-5 hours. Turn the pie plate upside down, pop the plaster and play dough out, and peel the dough off the plaster. You should see your "fossil" printed on the plaster.